You Can Solve It!

By Liz Ray

Scott Foresman
is an imprint of

Glenview, Illinois • Boston, Massachusetts • Chandler, Arizona •
Upper Saddle River, New Jersey

ISBN: 13: 978-0-328-46381-7
ISBN 10:   0-328-46381-7

Being messy is a problem.
You can clean up.

Being noisy is a problem.
You can be quiet.

Being late is a problem.

You can get ready early.

Being tired is a problem.
You can rest.

Being lost is a problem.
You can get help.

Being lonely is a problem.
You can make a friend.